Placing your bands

Make sure all your bands are in the correct place by following the band nun otherwise, your finished piece won't work. Sometimes, bands need to be p this is shown as two numbers on the band.

In most projects, a top band is placed as the last band, shown as a number the diagrams. Simply wrap the band around the designated peg twice. If a between more than one peg, this is shown in the diagrams as a double line

Threading beads

Beads can really make your project stand out from the crowd, but make sure the hole is big enough to thread your band through. If you're finding it tricky, take a paperclip, unfold it and leave just one bend in it. Then, thread one end of it through the band, and poke both ends of it through the bead, before bending the paperclip out (*Photo 3*).

Another cool technique we use in this guide is to wrap one band around another, which is then stretched between the pegs as normal. Simply take your first band and wrap it around your hook four times (*Photo 4*). Now, take your second band and catch it on the end of your hook (*Photo 5*). Carefully slide the first band off over the hook, so it's suspended on the second band (*Photo 6*). It takes a bit of practice, but once you've mastered it, it can be very useful!

Hooking and looping

Before you start hooking and looping, check your loom arrows are facing towards you. With a lot of our designs, the bands are hooked and looped in reverse order to how they were placed. A handy way to work out your looping pattern is to turn your diagram upside down, so its arrow faces the same way as your loom's arrows.

When hooking, always go inside the peg to take the band, unless the project states otherwise, and only catch the band(s) in question each time (*Photo 7*). When looping, try not to twist your bands, and stretch them off your hook and securely onto the peg (*Photo 8*). Simple!

Looping off

At the end of most projects, you need to secure them before taking them off the loom. This is done by either sliding the last two band ends on your hook and attaching them together with a clip (*Photo 9*) or by making a slipknot. When making a slipknot, you'll normally have two ends of the same band looped to the same peg (*Photo 10*). Going from inside the last peg, hook the bottom end of this band (*Photo 11*), then pull it up through itself (*Photo 12*). As you continue to pull on that end of the band, the slipknot will tighten and secure itself.

Extending

Some of our designs will need extending to fit. Simply place your remaining bands in a zigzag pattern, but place the end bands of your project as a top band on the last peg of your loom. You can then make a simple chain to the right length.

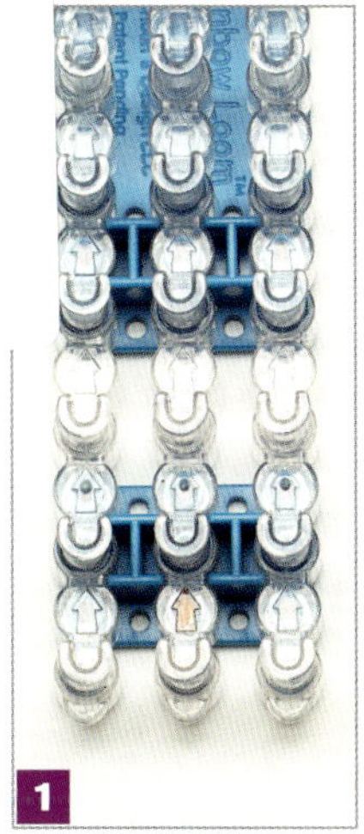
1

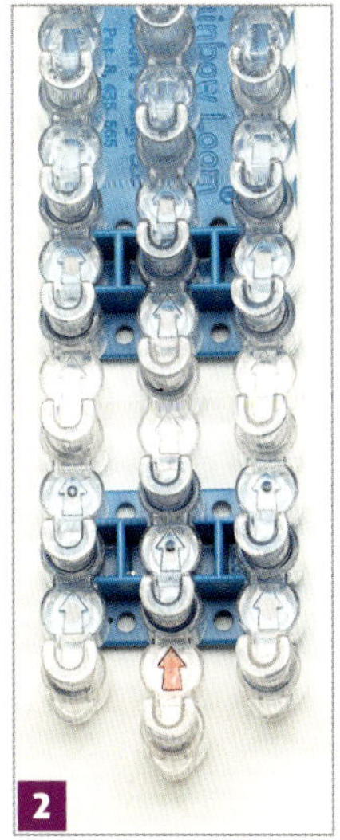
2

3

4

5

6

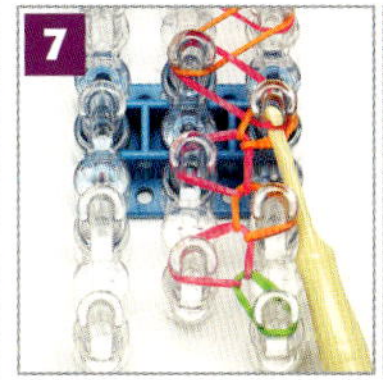
7

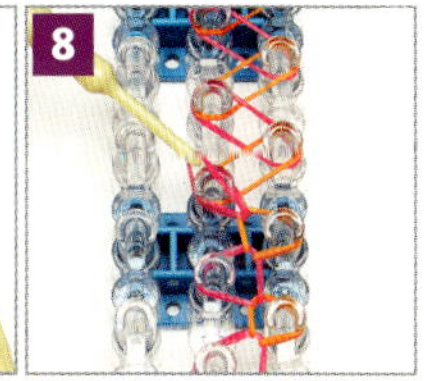
8

9

10

11

12

Animal Project One

Cat

For this project you'll need:

- ✓ 1 blue band
- ✓ 3 pink bands
- ✓ 4 black bands
- ✓ 29 orange bands
- ✓ 2 black eye beads
- ✓ Scissors

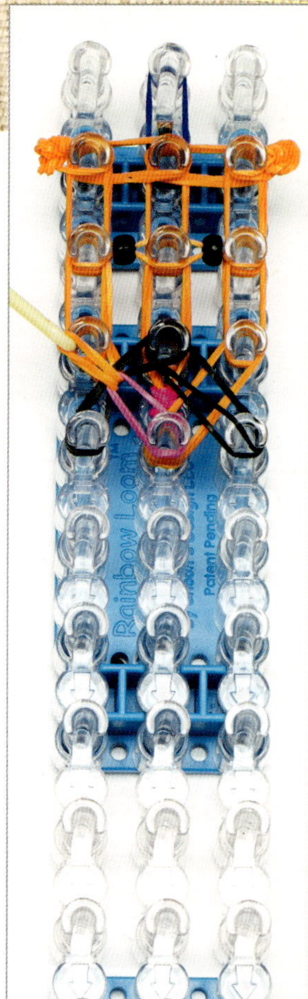

Setting up your loom!

Set up your loom in the SQUARED configuration, making sure the arrow is facing away from you, then place the bands in the order shown in the diagram. Before placing bands 6-7, you need to loop 8-9 around them. To do this, loop pink bands 8-9 around your hook four times, then catch 6-7 on the end of your hook, and carefully slide 8-9 off your hook and onto them (*see photo right*). Do the same to bands 32-37, using the diagram to help. These become the ears. Before placing band 31, thread it through two black beads and stretch it between the pegs as normal. These become the eyes.

1 Turn your loom so the arrow is facing towards you. With this design, you're going to be looping the bands in reverse order to how they were placed, starting at pink band 26. Put your hook in this peg, push back the pink band, hook the first pair of orange bands and loop them diagonally to the upper left-hand side.

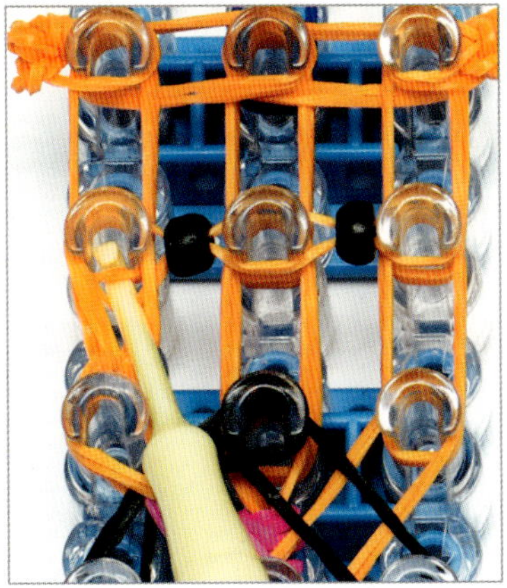

2 Continue hooking and looping the next two pairs of orange bands in this row, making sure you always hook from inside the peg and only catch the bottom pair of bands each time.

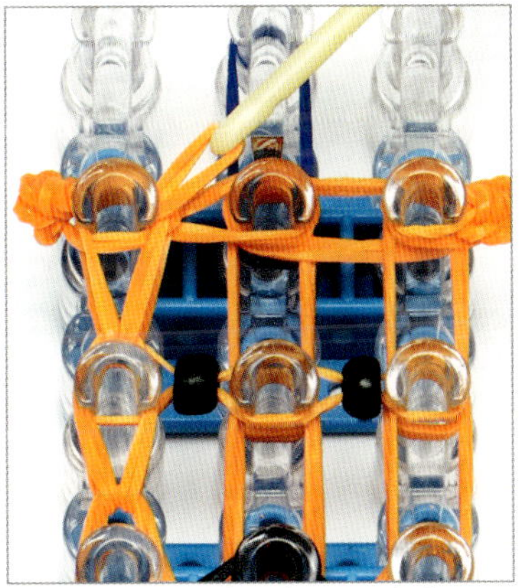

3 When you go to loop the next pair of bands, hook them from the bottom of the peg as normal, but loop them horizontally to the central row.

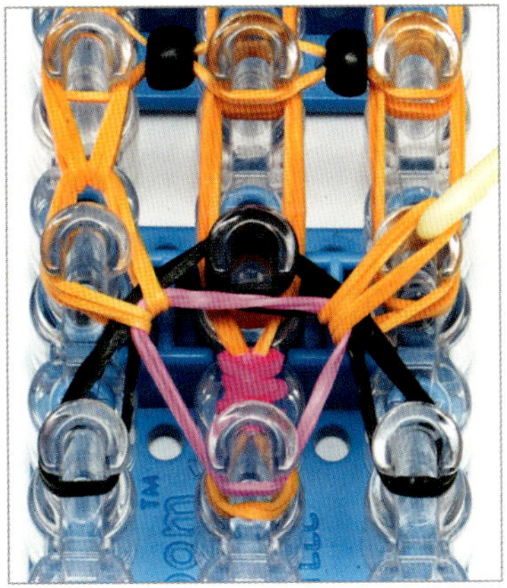

4 Repeat steps 1-3 on the right-hand side, starting by looping the next pair of orange bands from under pink band 26 diagonally to the upper right-hand peg.

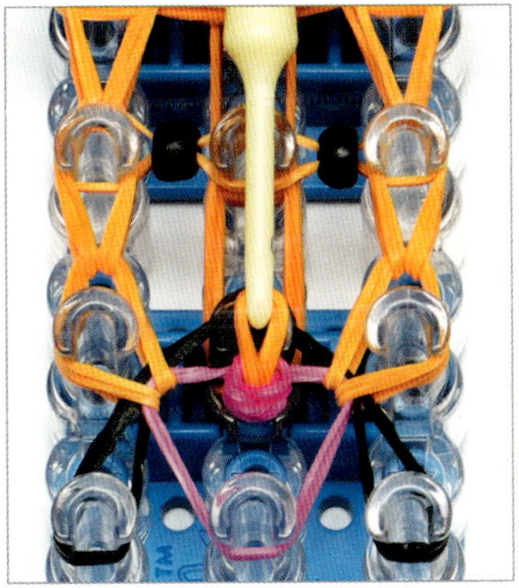

5 Once more, go back to the peg with pink band 26 on it, reach underneath to hook the bottom pair of orange bands and loop them forward.

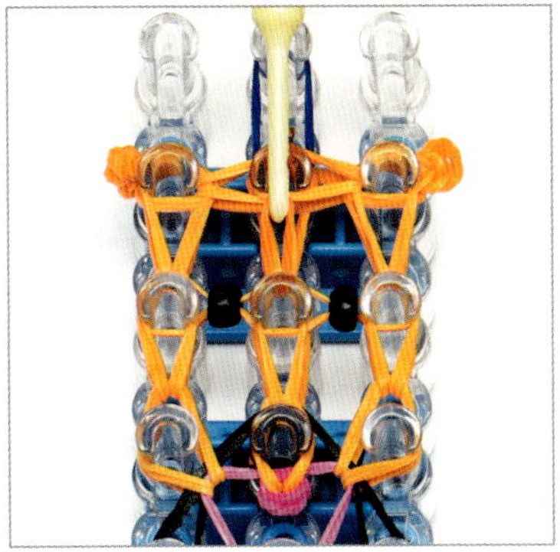

6 Continue hooking and looping the next two pairs of orange bands forward.

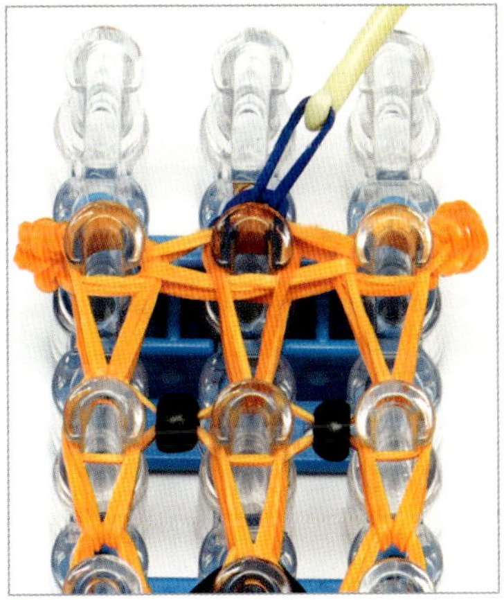

7 Now, put your hook in the peg you just finished on, reach down and catch the bottom blue band. Loop it forward, then pull the bottom end of it up through itself to create a slipknot.

8 Gently pull the bands off the loom.

9 To make your whiskers, take the two black bands on the left and tie them tightly together. Repeat on the right.

10 Now, snip the two black loops on each side to reveal your whiskers. Meow!

Animal Project Two

Snake

For this project you'll need:

- ✓ 1 pink band
- ✓ 37 green bands
- ✓ 19 orange bands
- ✓ 2 black eye beads
- ✓ Scissors

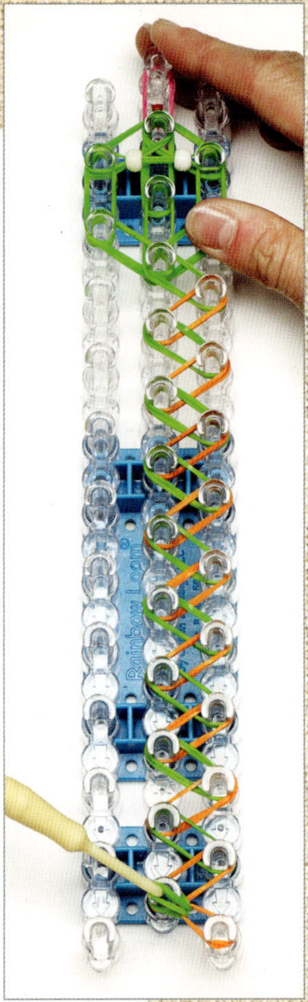

Setting up your loom!

Set up your loom in the STAGGERED configuration, making sure the arrow is facing away from you, then place the bands in the order shown in the diagram. Before placing band 57, thread it through the two beads, before stretching it between the pegs as normal. These become the eyes.

1 Turn your loom so the arrow is facing towards you. With this design, you're going to be looping the bands in reverse order to how they were placed, starting at orange band 56. Put your hook in this peg, push back the orange band, hook the bottom pair of green bands and loop them diagonally to the upper left-hand side.

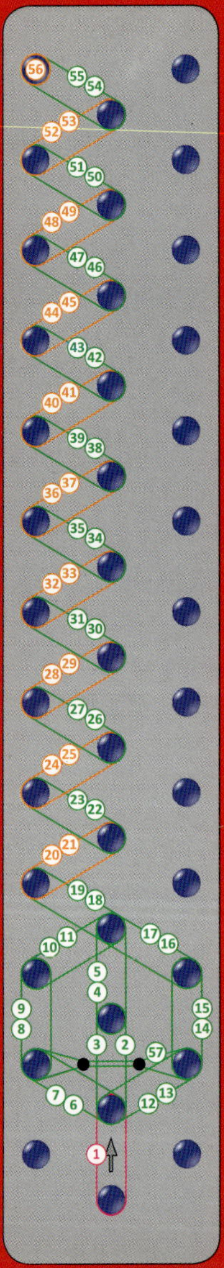

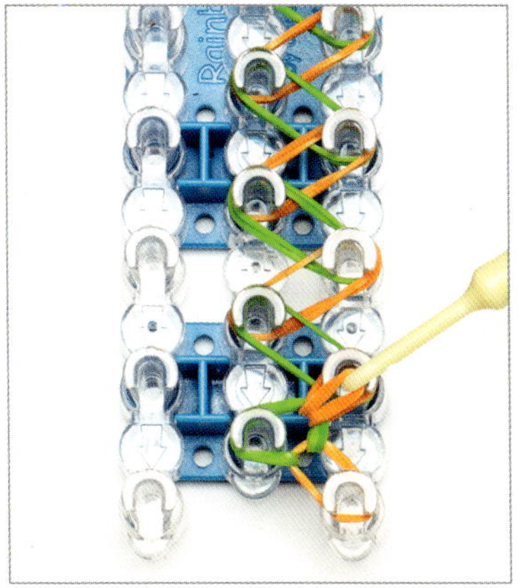

2 Putting your hook in the peg you just looped to, catch the bottom pair of orange bands and loop them diagonally to the upper right-hand peg.

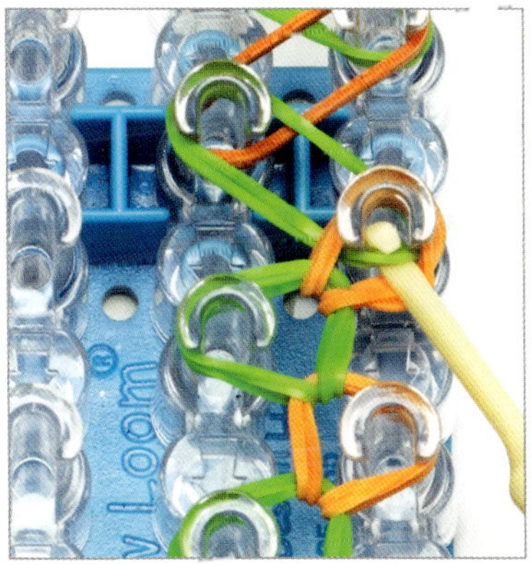

3 Continue hooking and looping the next 17 pairs of green and orange bands in this zigzag pattern, making sure you always hook from inside the peg and only catch the bottom pair of bands each time.

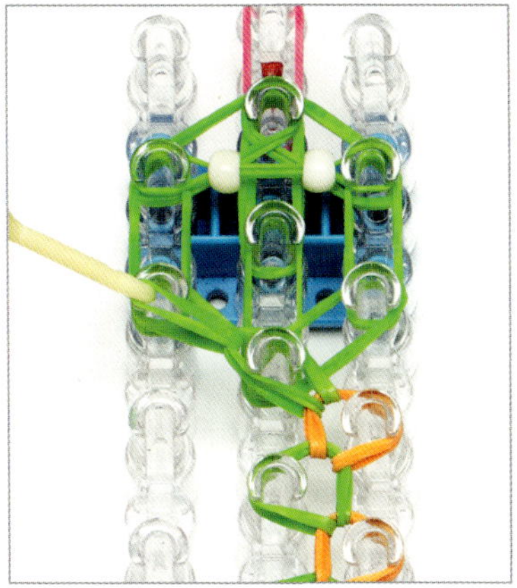

4 You've now reached the head. When you go to loop the next pair of bands, hook the second green pair down from the peg and loop them diagonally to the upper left-hand side.

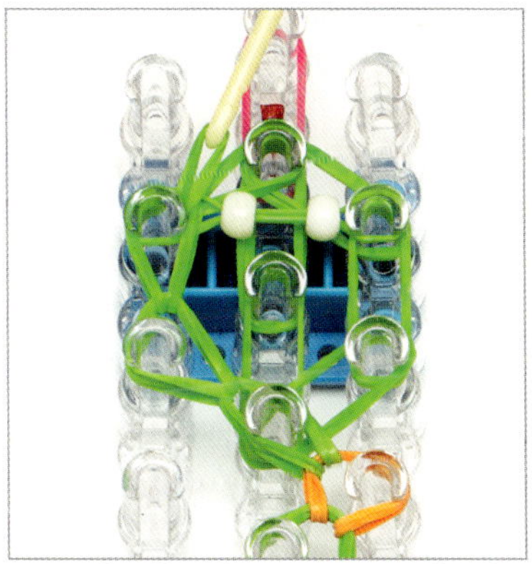

5 Hook and loop the next two pairs of bands in this row in the same way, starting at the peg you just looped to. Note that the second pair of bands will be looped diagonally to the upper central peg.

6 Go back to the start of the snake's head and repeat steps 4-5 on the right-hand side.

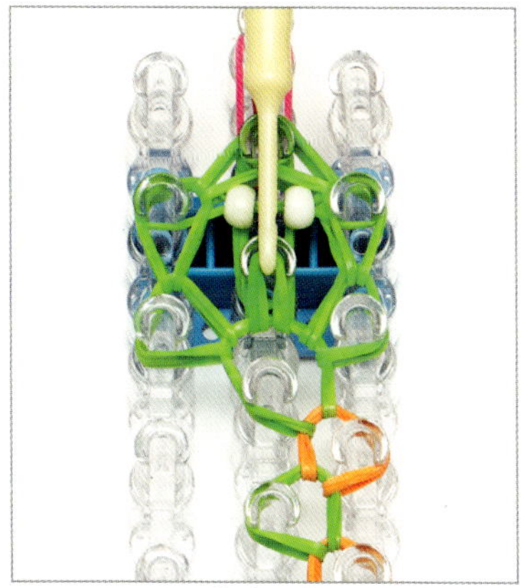

7 Once more, go back to the start of the snake's head, this time hooking the bottom pair of green bands and looping them forward.

8 Hook and loop the next pair of green bands forward.

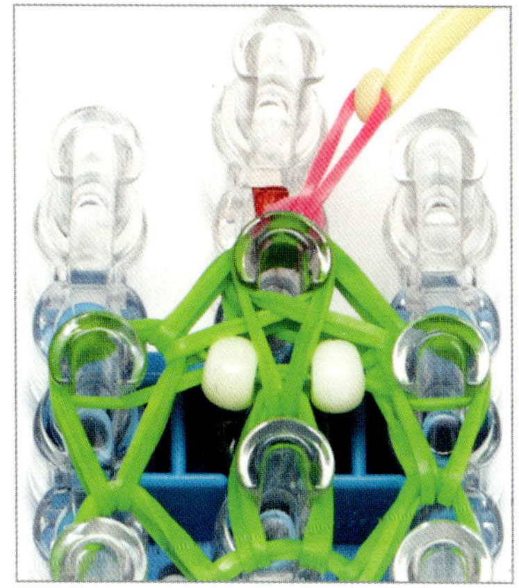

9 Now, put your hook in the peg you just finished on, reach down and catch the bottom pink band. Loop it forward, then pull the bottom end of it up through itself to create a slipknot.

10 Slither your snake off the loom, then tie a little knot in the pink band and cut the looped end to make a forked snake's tongue. Sssssplendid!

Bracelet Project One

Beady Wonder

For this project you'll need:

- ✓ 14 black bands
- ✓ 2 red bands
- ✓ 2 orange bands
- ✓ 2 yellow bands
- ✓ 2 green bands
- ✓ 2 blue bands
- ✓ 2 pink bands
- ✓ 13 black beads
- ✓ 1 clip

Setting up your loom!

Set up your loom in the STAGGERED configuration, making sure the arrow is facing away from you, then place the bands in the order shown in the diagram. Before placing the black bands, you have to thread all but one through a black bead first (*see photo below*), then stretch them between the pegs as normal.

1 Turn your loom so the arrow is facing towards you. With this design, you're going to be looping the bands in reverse order to how they were placed, starting with black band 26. So, putting your hook inside this peg, push back the top band, hook the bottom black band and loop it diagonally to the upper left-hand peg.

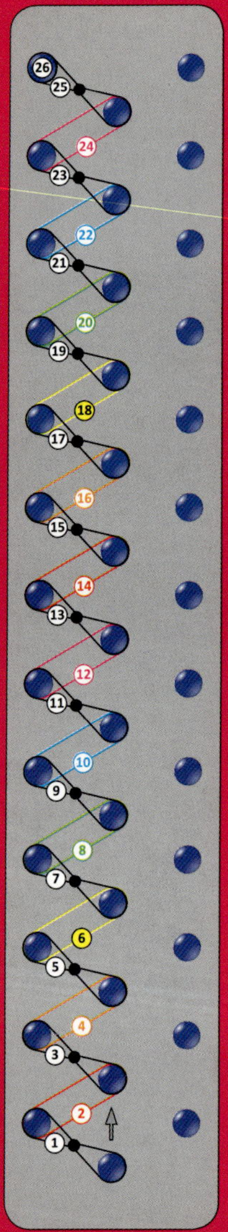

2 Putting your hook back in the peg you just looped to, catch the pink band from inside and loop it diagonally to the peg on the upper right-hand side.

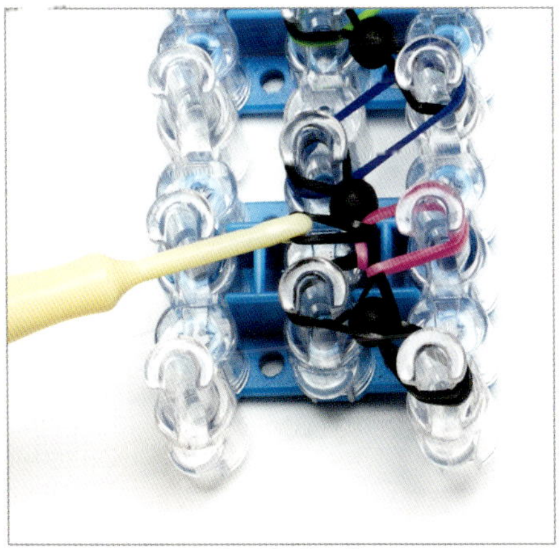

3 Now, putting your hook back in the peg you just looped to, catch the black band from inside and loop it diagonally to the peg on the upper left-hand side.

4 Keep hooking and looping in this zigzag pattern, counting down in reverse numerical order, to the end of the loom. Make sure you always hook the bottom band from inside the other bands on the peg.

5 Once you're at the end of the loom, slide both ends of the last band off the last peg and onto your hook. Now, slide your clip onto both of them to attach them together.

6 Still using your hook as support, pull all the bands off the loom. Then, to complete your bracelet, attach both loops of the black band from the other end of the chain to the clip as well. Your beady bracelet is now ready to wear!

Bracelet Project Two

Flower Bracelet

Setting up your loom!

Set up your loom in the STAGGERED configuration, making sure the arrow is facing away from you, then place the bands in the order shown in the diagram.

1 Turn your loom so the arrow is facing towards you. With this design, you're going to be looping the bands in reverse order to how they were placed, starting at orange band 34. So, putting your hook inside this peg, push back the top orange band, hook the top pink band and loop it diagonally to the upper left-hand peg, where it originates from.

For this project you'll need:

- ✓ 1 orange band
- ✓ 3 purple bands
- ✓ 3 pink bands
- ✓ 27 green bands
- ✓ 1 clip

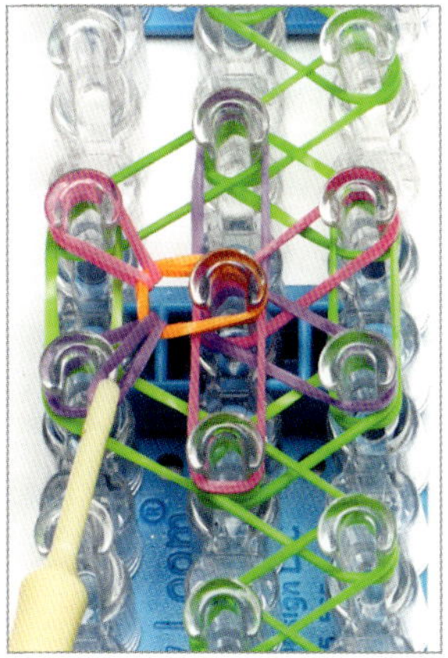

2 Go back to the central peg, push back the orange top band, hook the first purple band and loop it diagonally to the lower left-hand peg, where it originates from.

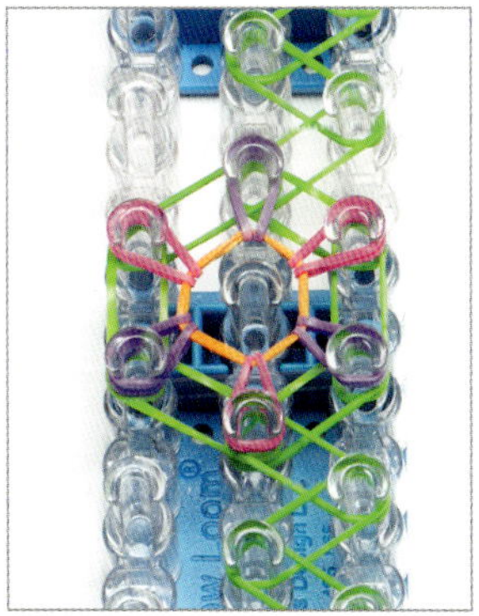

3 Continue looping the remaining four pink and purple bands in this way in an anticlockwise direction, until the central orange band is evenly stretched between the six pegs.

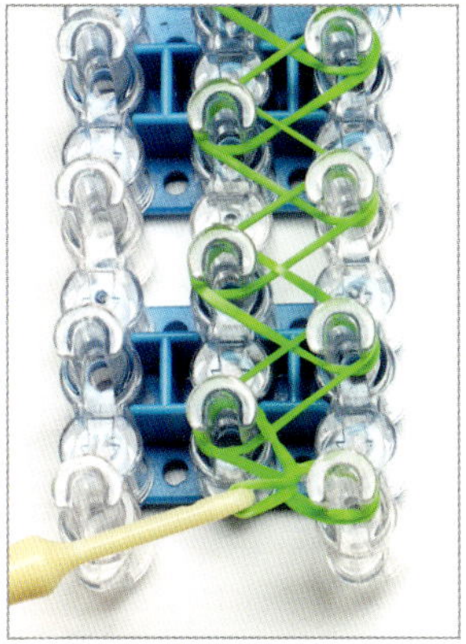

4 You're now ready to loop the green bands. Put your hook in the peg with the green band 27 on, push back the top band, hook the bottom band and loop it diagonally to the peg on the upper left-hand side.

5 Put your hook inside the peg you just looped to, catch the bottom green band and loop it diagonally to the upper right-hand side.

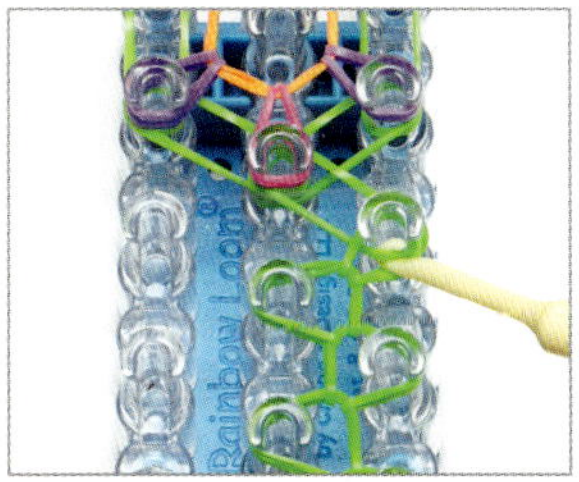

6 Keep hooking and looping in this zigzag pattern, counting down in reverse numerical order for a further nine bands. Make sure you always hook the bottom band from inside the other bands on the peg.

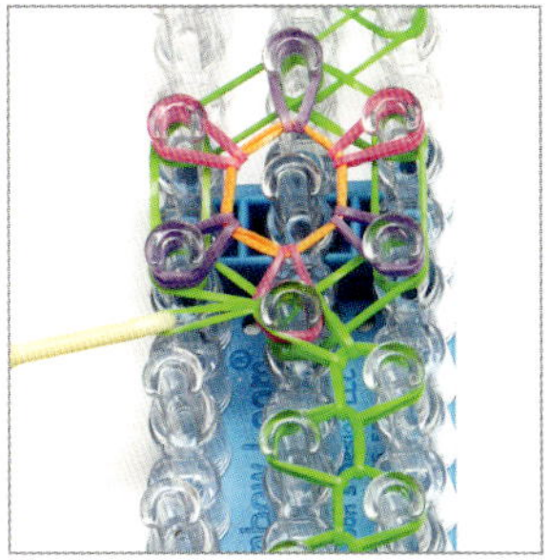

7 You've now reached the flower. Put your hook in the peg you just looped to, reach down, past the pink bands, to the green band that's second from bottom. Hook it and loop it diagonally to the upper left-hand peg.

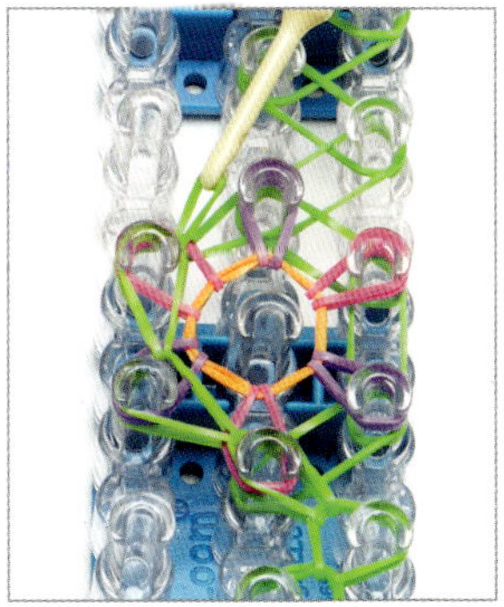

8 Hook and loop the next two green bands in order, starting at the peg you just looped to. Note that the second one will be looped diagonally to the central row.

9 Go back to the start of the flower, put your hook inside past the pink band, catch the very bottom green band and loop it diagonally to the upper right-hand side.

10 Hook and loop the next two green bands in order, starting at the peg you just looped to. Note that the second band will be looped diagonally to the central row.

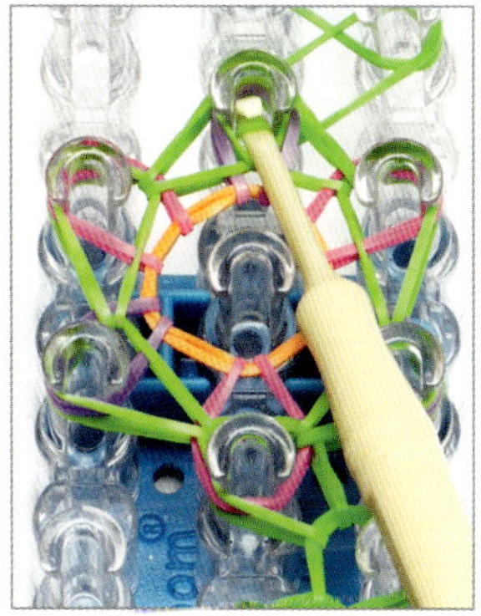

11 Putting your hook in the peg you just looped to, catch the very bottom green band and loop it diagonally to the upper right-hand peg.

12 Continue looping the remaining eight green bands in a zigzag pattern, always hooking from inside the other bands.

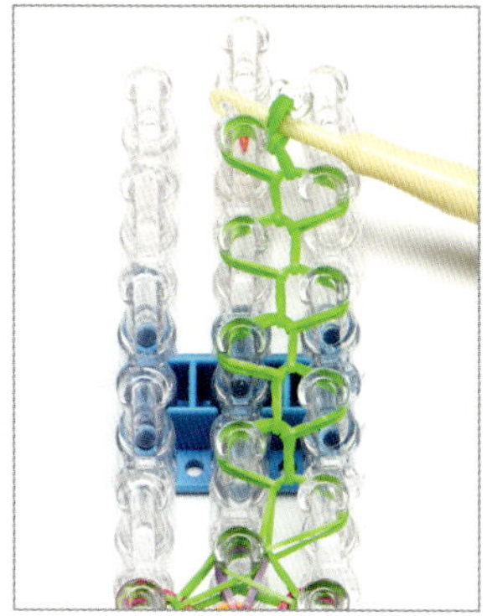

13 Once you're at the end of the loom, slide both ends of the last band off the last peg and onto your hook. Now, slide your clip onto both of them to attach them together.

14 Still using your hook as support, pull all the bands off the loom. Then, to complete your bracelet, attach both loops of the black band from the other end of the chain into the clip as well. Flower-tastic!

Fruit Project One

Cherries

For this project you'll need:

- ✓ 2 green bands
- ✓ 34 red bands

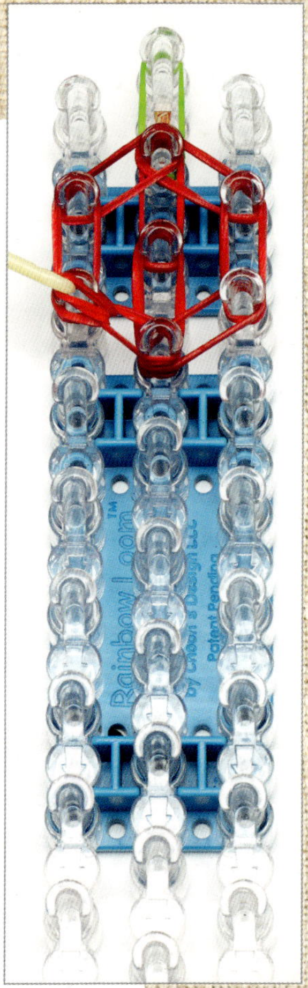

Setting up your loom!

Set up your loom in the STAGGERED configuration, making sure the arrow is facing away from you, then place the bands in the order shown in the diagram. You're going to need to place the bands like this twice to make two cherries.

1 Turn your loom so the arrow is facing towards you. We're going to be looping the bands in reverse order to how they were placed, starting at band 18. Put your hook inside the peg, push back the top band, hook the next pair of bands and loop them diagonally to their original peg on the left-hand side.

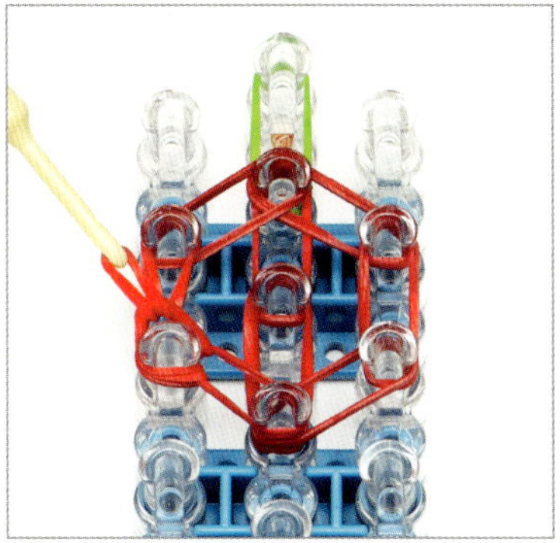

2 Put your hook inside the peg you just ended on, hook the bottom pair of bands and loop them forward.

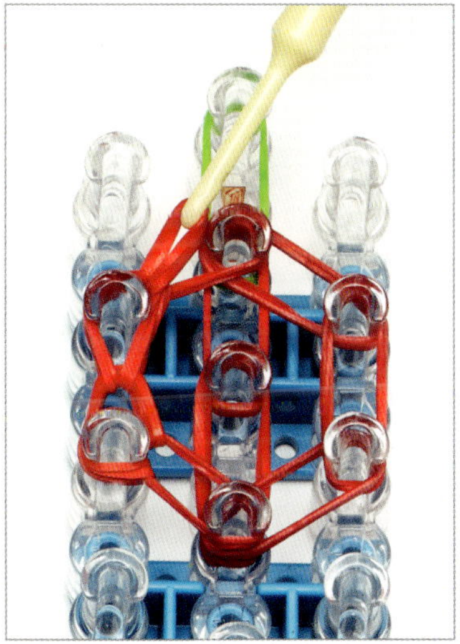

3 Now, put your hook inside the peg you just ended on, hook the bottom pair of bands and loop them diagonally to the upper central peg.

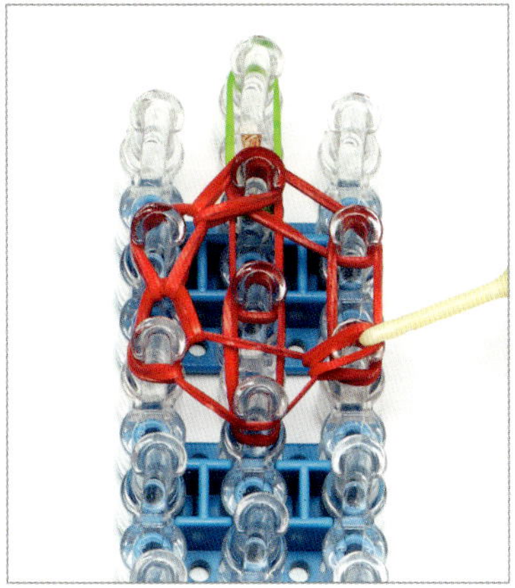

4 Going back to the first peg, where band 18 had been placed, put your hook inside the peg, push back the top band, hook the next pair of bands down and loop them to their original peg on the right-hand side.

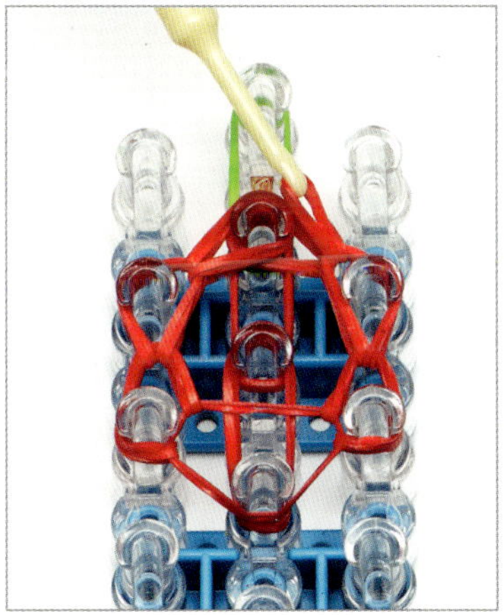

5 Repeat steps 2-3 on the right-hand side.

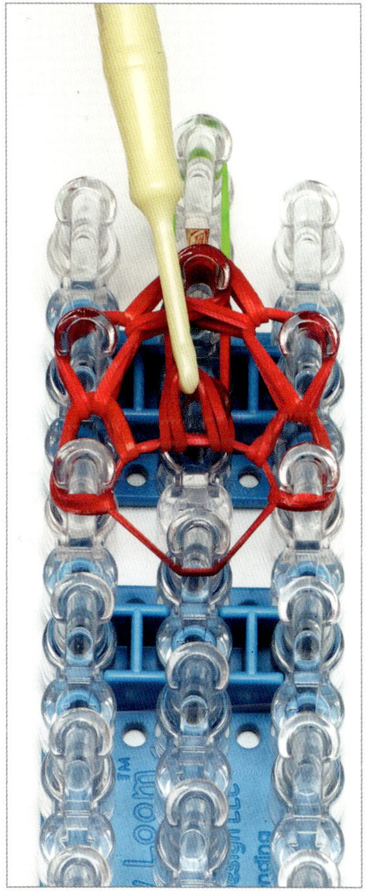

6 Once more, go back to the first peg, where band 18 had been placed, put your hook inside the peg, push back the top band, hook the bottom pair of red bands and loop them forward.

7 Now, loop the next pair of bands forward, too.

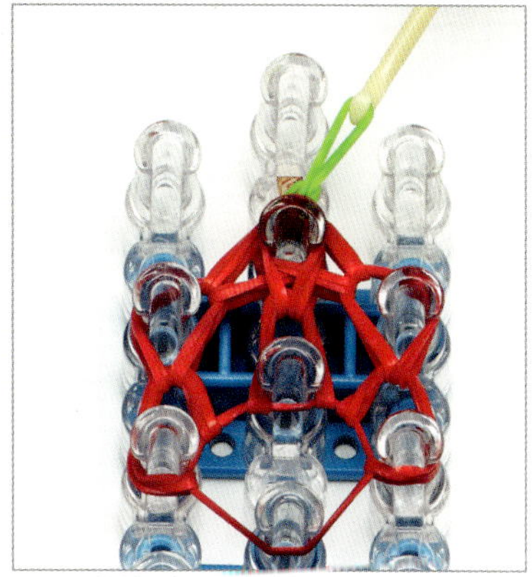

8 To finish off your first cherry, put your hook inside the peg you just ended on, hook the last single green band and loop it forward. Now, catch the bottom end of it and pull it up through itself to create a slipknot.

For extra help on casting off and slipknots, see p3. Pull your first cherry off the loom.

9 Now, making sure your loom arrow is facing away from you, place the rest of your bands on the loom using the diagram. Repeat steps 1-8 to make your second cherry.

10 To attach your cherries together, thread one of the green band stalks through the other green band, then stretch it over its own cherry to create a slipknot. Your cherries are now complete! They make a lovely charm!

Fruit Project Two

Banana

For this project you'll need:

- ✔ 4 black bands
- ✔ 23 yellow bands

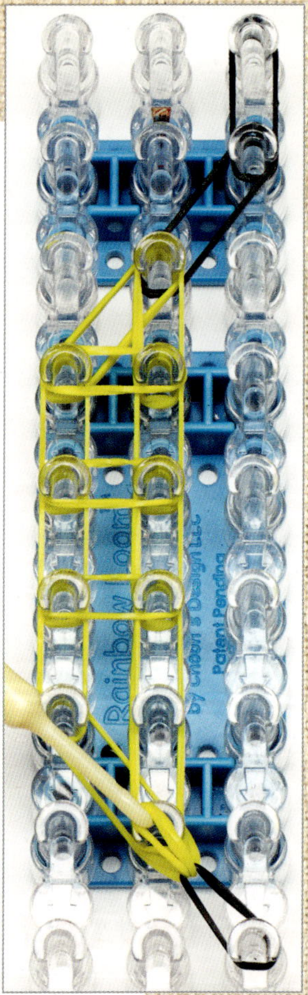

Setting up your loom!

Set up your loom in the SQUARED configuration, making sure the arrow is facing away from you, then place the bands in the order shown in the diagram. Note that bands 25-27 are wrapped around the pegs twice.

1 Turn your loom so the arrow is facing towards you. We're going to be looping the bands in reverse order to how they were placed, starting at black band 24. Put your hook inside the peg, push back the black top band, hook the first pair of yellow bands and loop them diagonally to their original peg on the left-hand side.

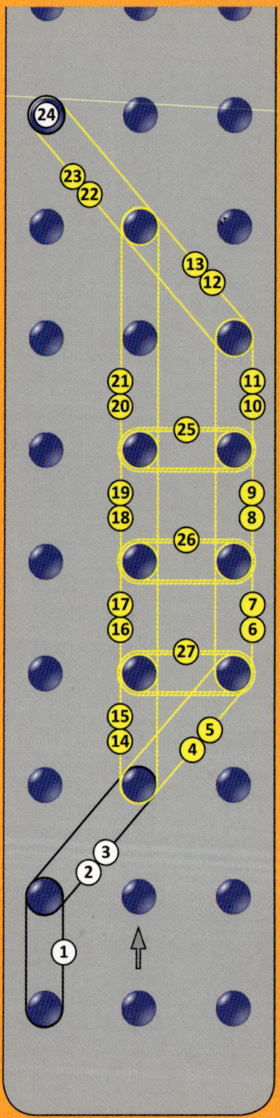

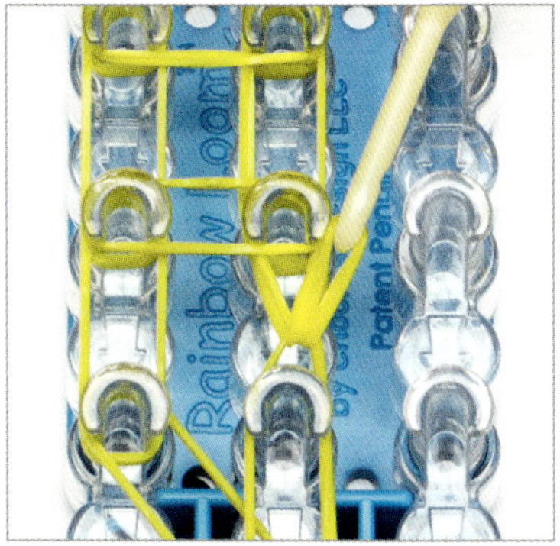

2 Put your hook inside the peg you just ended on, hook the first pair of yellow bands and loop them forward to their original peg. Note that you'll be skipping past one peg to do so – this gives the banana its bend!

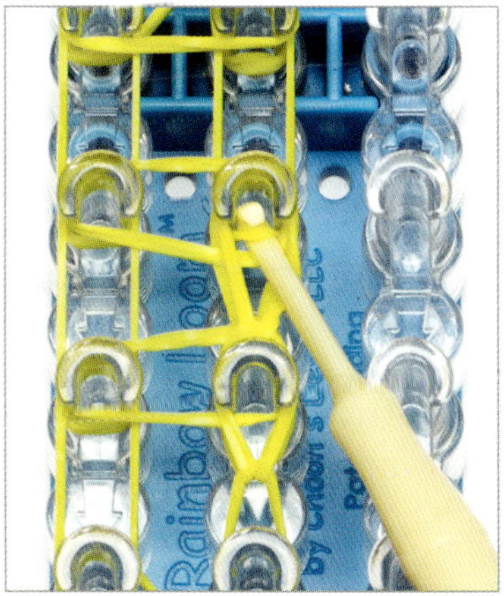

3 Hook and loop the next three pairs of yellow bands in this row, making sure each time you go inside the peg and only take the bottom pair of bands.

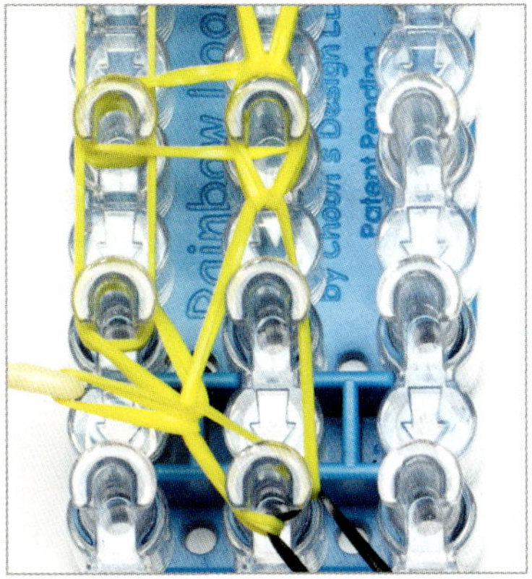

4 Going back to the first used central peg, put your hook back inside the peg, catch the bottom pair of yellow bands and loop them diagonally to their original peg on the upper left-hand side.

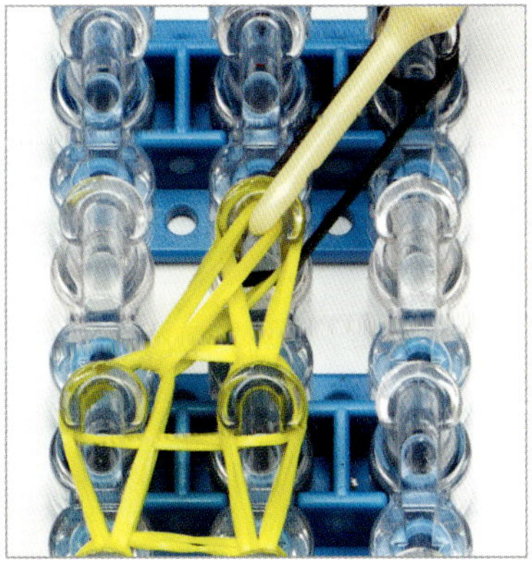

5 Hook and loop the next four pairs of yellow bands, making sure each time you go inside the peg and only take the bottom pair of bands. Note that the fourth pair you hook will be looped diagonally to the upper central peg.

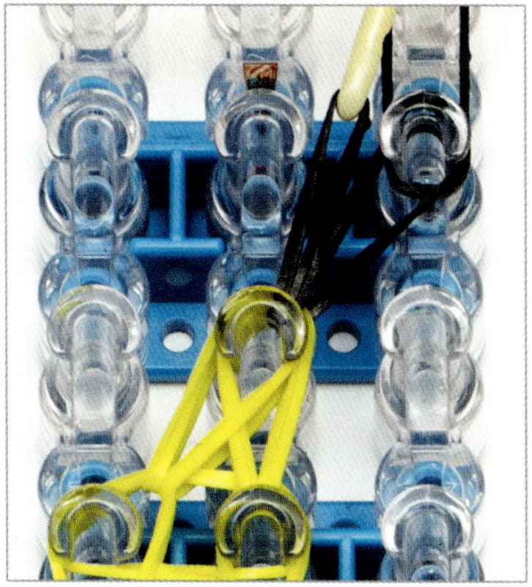

6 Now, put your hook inside the peg you just finished on, catch the bottom pair of black bands and loop them diagonally to the upper left-hand peg.

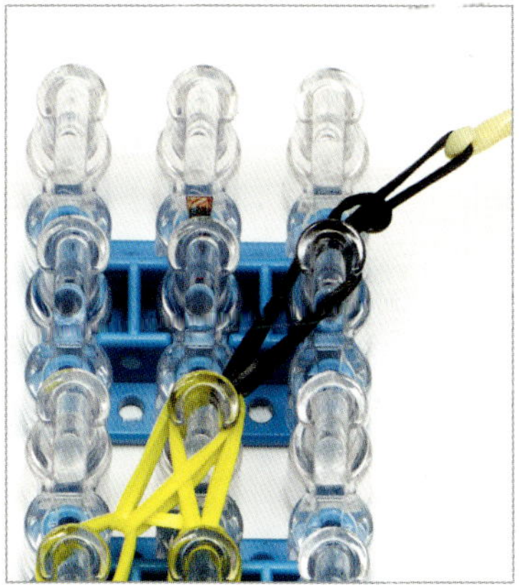

7 To finish off your banana, put your hook inside the peg you just ended on, hook the last single black band and loop it forward. Now, catch the bottom end of it and pull it up through itself to create a slipknot.

8 Carefully peel your fruit off the loom – top banana!

Rings Project One

Diamond

For this project you'll need:

- ✓ 7 pink bands
- ✓ 8 purple bands
- ✓ 1 clip

Setting up your loom!

Set up your loom in the STAGGERED configuration, making sure the arrow is facing away from you, then place the bands in the order shown in the diagram.

1 Turn your loom so the arrow is facing towards you. With this design, you're going to be looping the bands in reverse order to how they were placed, starting with pink band 15. So, putting your hook inside this peg, push back the top band, hook the bottom pink band and loop it forward.

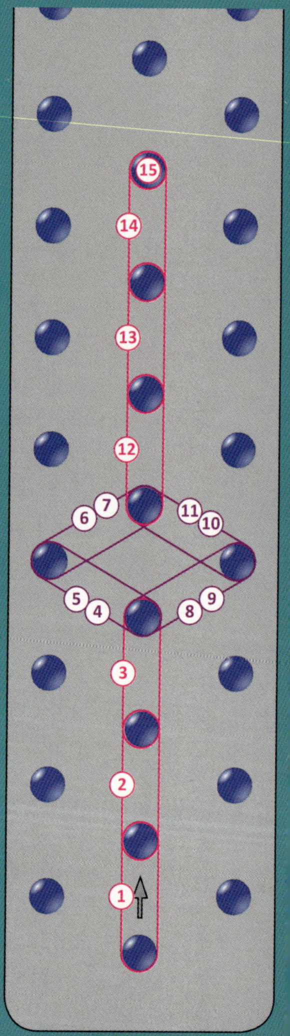

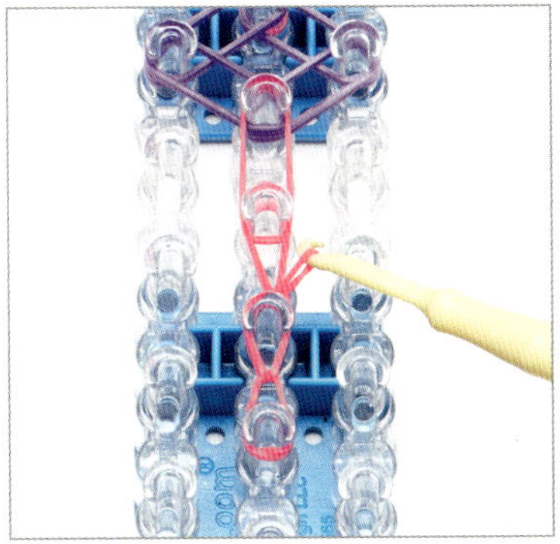

2 At the peg you just looped to, put your hook inside, catch the bottom pink band and loop it forward.

3 Repeat step 2 with the next pink band.

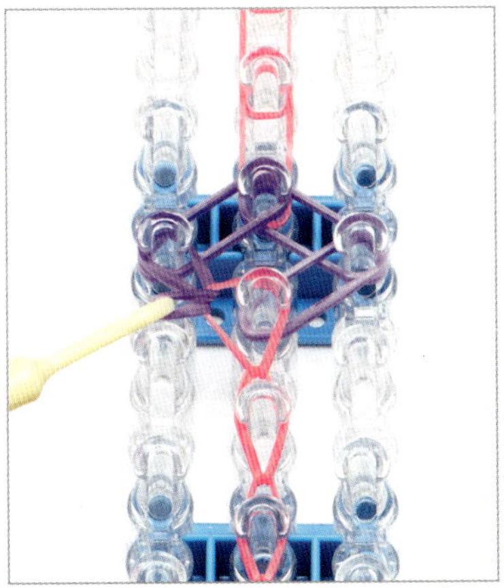

4 Now, putting your hook in the peg you just finished on, catch the top pair of purple bands and loop them diagonally to the upper left-hand side peg.

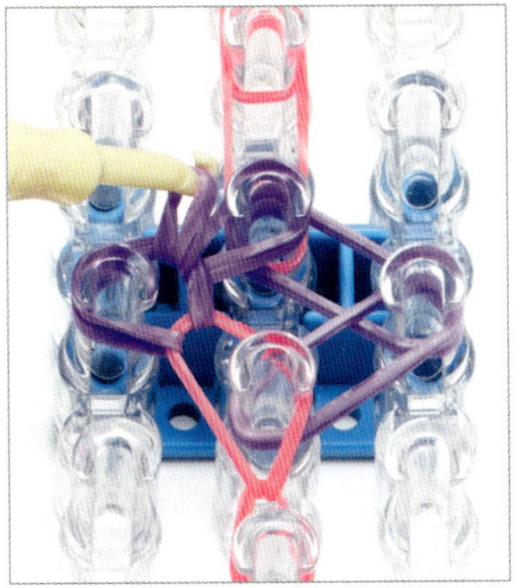

5 Now, at the peg you just looped to, hook the bottom pair of purple bands and loop them diagonally to the upper central peg.

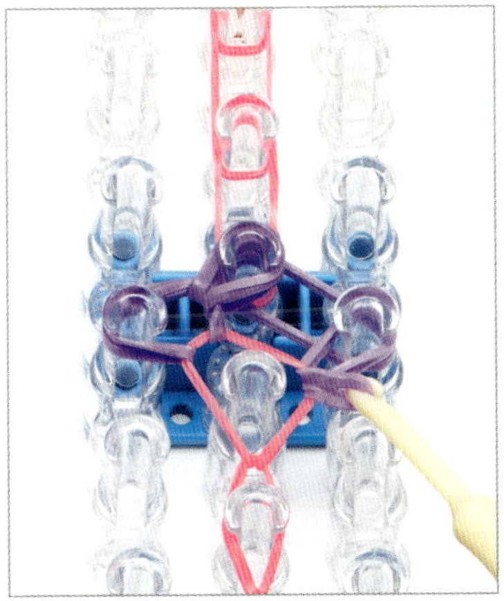

6 Going back inside the peg where the purple bands started, catch the bottom pair of purple bands and loop them diagonally to the upper right-hand side peg.

7 Now, at the peg you just looped to, hook the bottom pair of purple bands and loop them diagonally to the upper central peg.

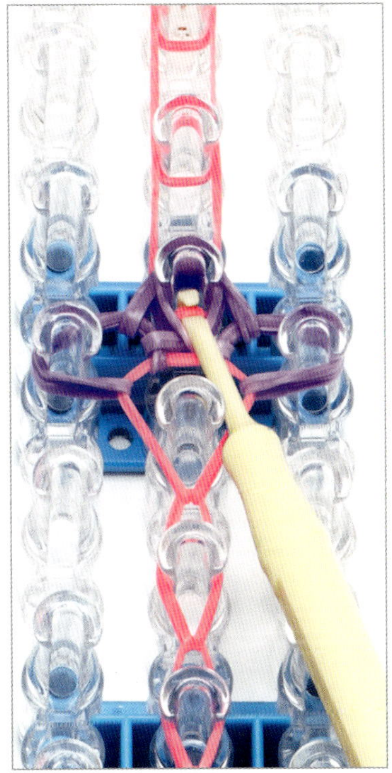

8 This next step takes a bit of care: put your hook inside the peg you just looped to and reach right down inside to catch the bottom pink band. When you've got it, loop it forward to the peg in front.

9 Loop the next two pink bands in the chain in the same way, so that you reach the end of the loom.

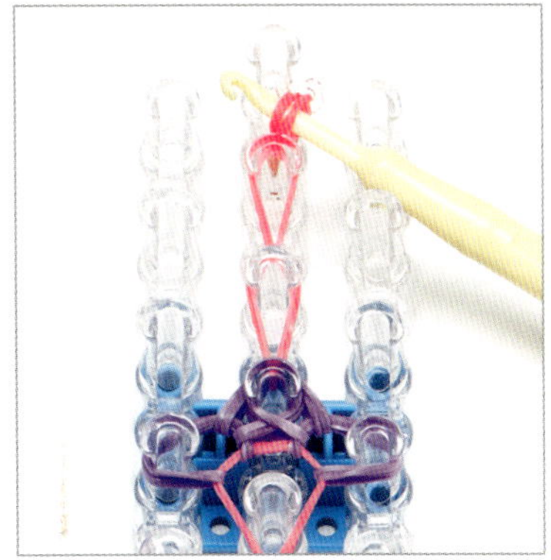

10 Slide both ends of the last band off the last peg and onto your hook. Now, slide your clip onto both of them to attach them together.

11 Pull all the bands off the loom. Then, to complete your ring, attach both loops of the last pink band from the other end of the chain into the clip as well. Gorgeous!

Rings Project Two

Trinal

For this project you'll need:

- ✔ 7 white bands
- ✔ 4 orange bands
- ✔ 4 yellow bands
- ✔ 4 blue bands
- ✔ 1 clip

Setting up your loom!

Set up your loom in the SQUARED configuration, making sure the arrow is facing away from you, then place the bands in the order shown in the diagram.

1 Turn your loom so the arrow is facing towards you. With this design, you're going to be looping the blue bands first, followed by the orange bands, then yellow, then white. You'll do this in reverse order to how they were placed, starting at band 16. So, putting your hook inside that peg, push back the top white band, catch the blue band and loop it diagonally to the upper left-hand peg.

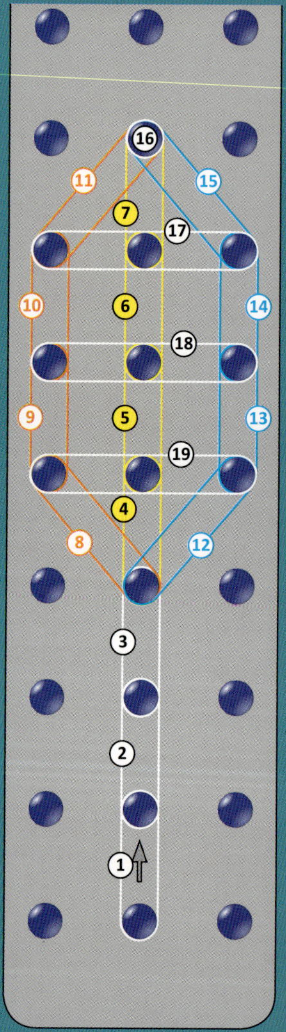

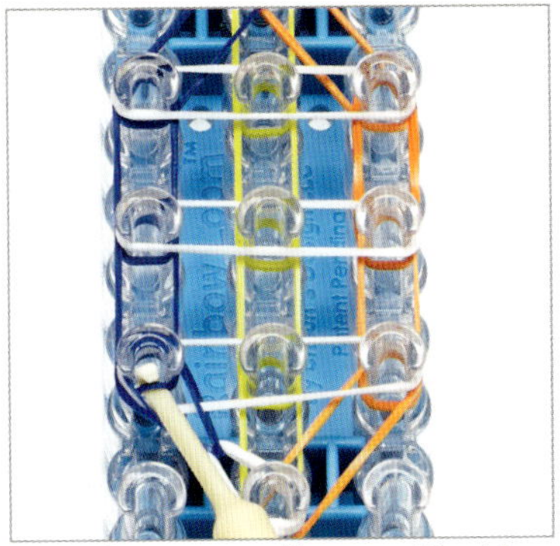

2 At the next peg, making sure not to catch the white band, hook the bottom blue band from inside and loop it forward, too.

3 Repeat step 2 with the next blue band.

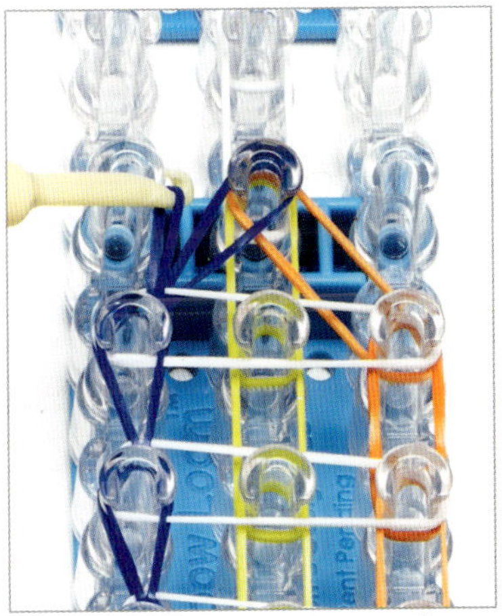

4 At the peg you just looped to, go inside as normal, catch the bottom blue band, but this time loop diagonally to the upper central peg.

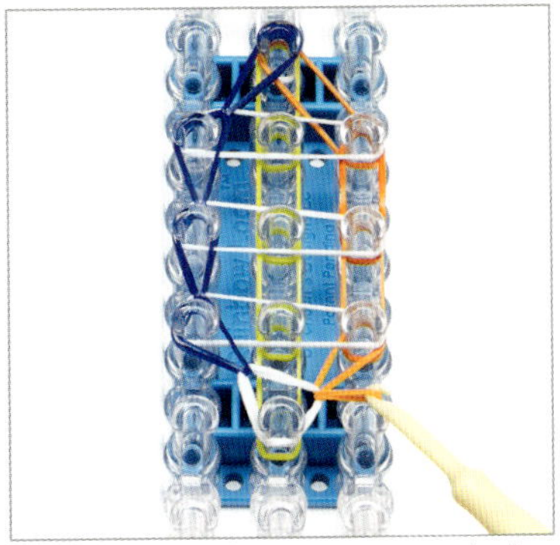

5 Going back to the start peg, put your hook inside, push back the top white band, hook the orange band and loop diagonally to the upper right-hand peg.

6 At the next peg, making sure not to catch the white band, hook the bottom orange band from inside and loop it forward, too.

7 Repeat step 6 with the next orange band.

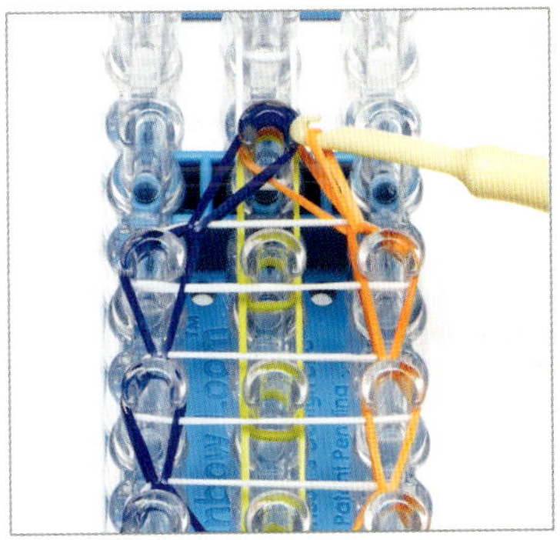

8 At the peg you just looped to, go inside as normal, catch the bottom orange band, but this time loop diagonally to the upper central peg.

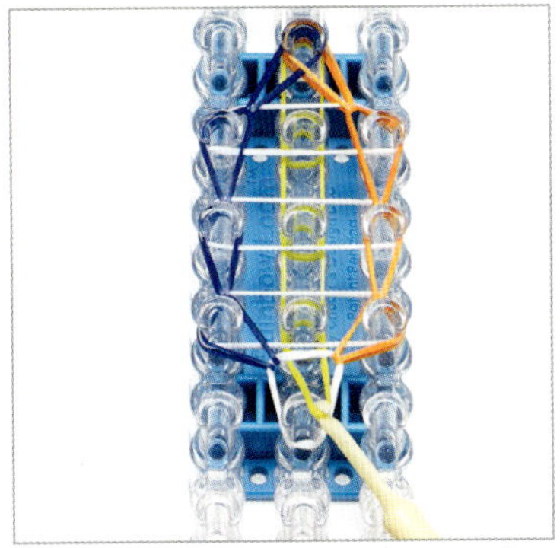

9 Once more, go back to the start peg, push back the top white band, hook the yellow band and loop it forward.

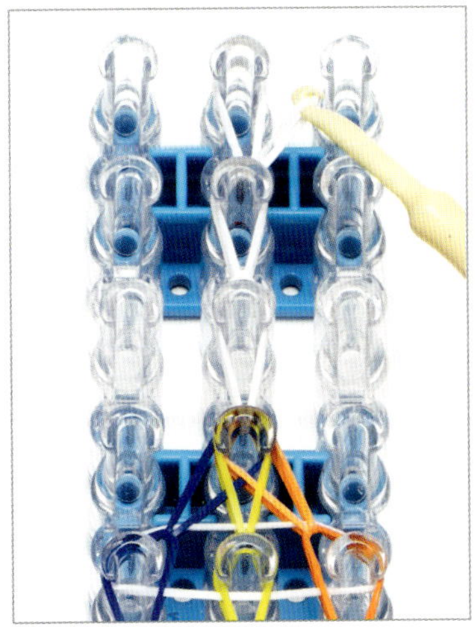

10 Hook and loop the remaining three yellow bands forward in the same way, before hooking and looping the last three white bands forward, too.

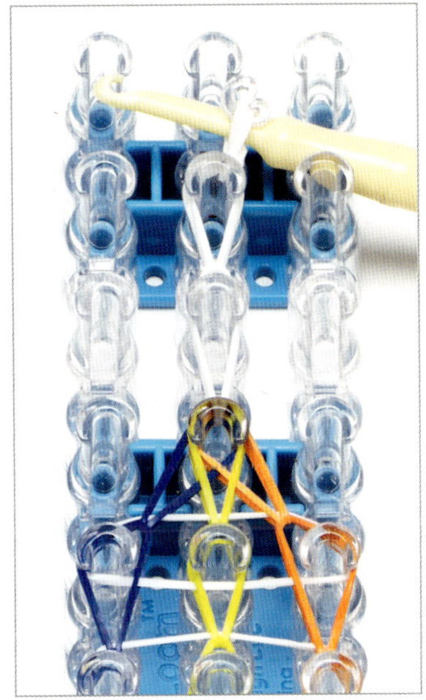

11 Slide the band ends from the last peg onto your hook, then join them together with a clip.

12 Pull all the bands off the loom. Now, to complete your ring, attach the white band from the other end of the chain to the clip as well. Your ring is ready to wear!

Headband Project One

Crown

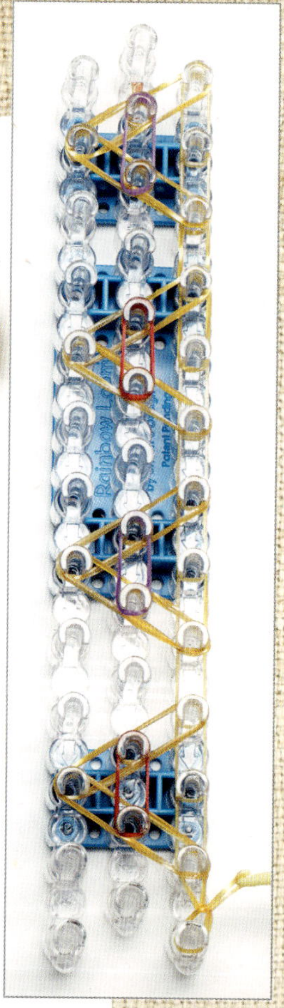

Setting up your loom!

Set up your loom in the STAGGERED configuration, making sure the arrow is facing away from you, then place the bands in the order shown in the diagram. You're going to place the bands like this twice to get the crown long enough.

For this project you'll need:

- ✓ 89 yellow/gold bands
- ✓ 4 red bands
- ✓ 4 purple bands
- ✓ 1 clip

1 Turn your loom so the arrow is facing towards you. You're going to start at gold band 13. Put your hook inside this peg, push back the top gold band, hook the bottom gold band and loop it forward.

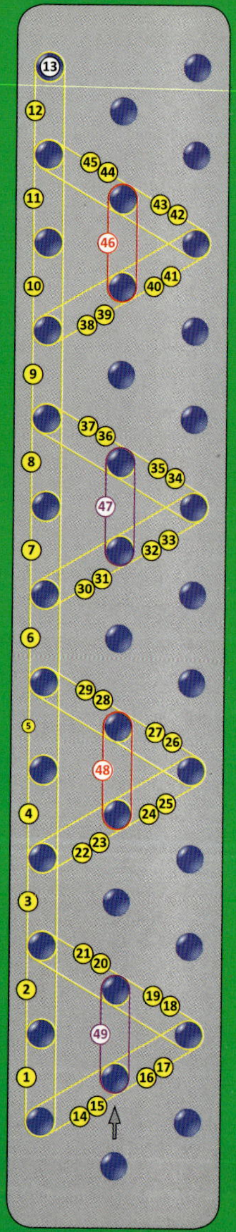

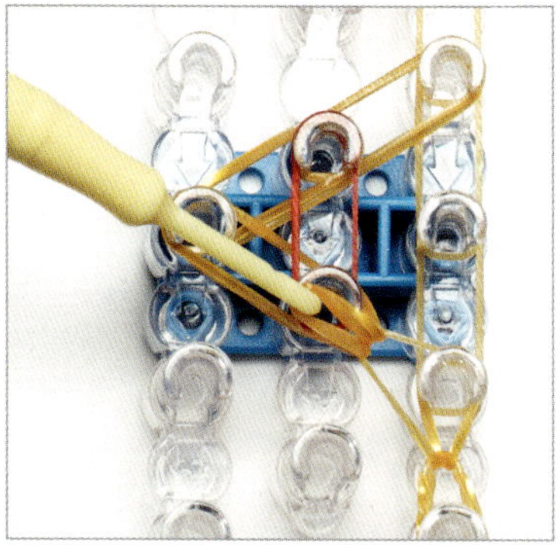

2 Put your hook inside the peg you just looped to, then under the top band take the first pair of gold bands and loop them diagonally to the upper left-hand peg.

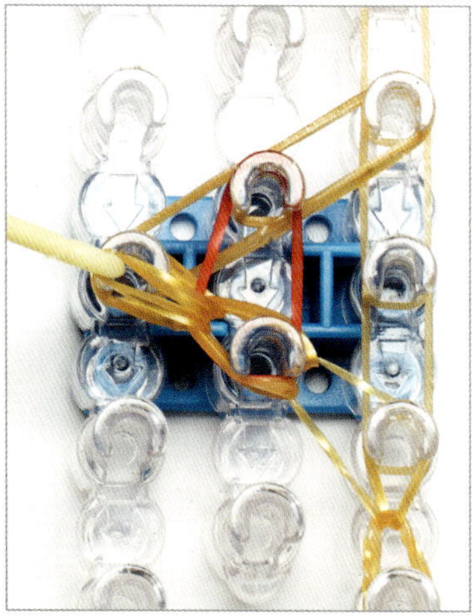

3 Now, at the peg you just looped to, go inside the red band, catch the bottom pair of gold bands and loop them diagonally to the upper left-hand peg.

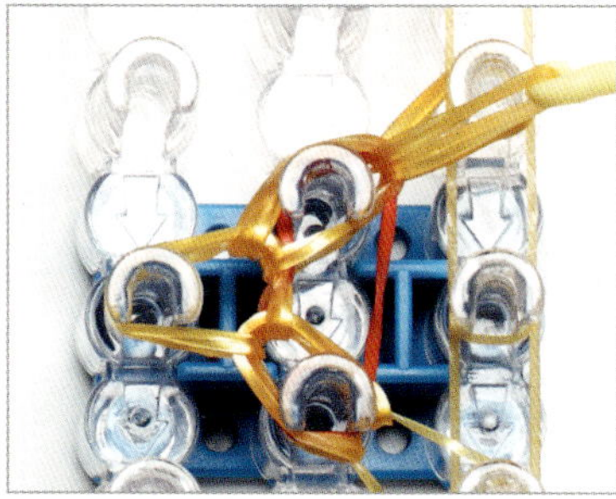

4 Loop the next two pairs of gold bands diagonally to the upper right-hand side, starting at the peg you just finished on and making sure you always loop from inside the peg.

5 Now, go back to the second peg in the right-hand row, hook the bottom gold band and loop it forward.

6 Loop the next two gold bands forward, making sure you always loop from inside the peg.

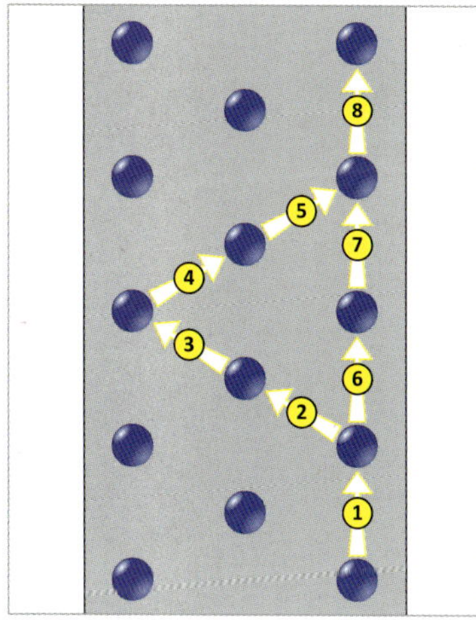

7 Continue looping in this pattern to the end of the loom, using this diagram to remind you.

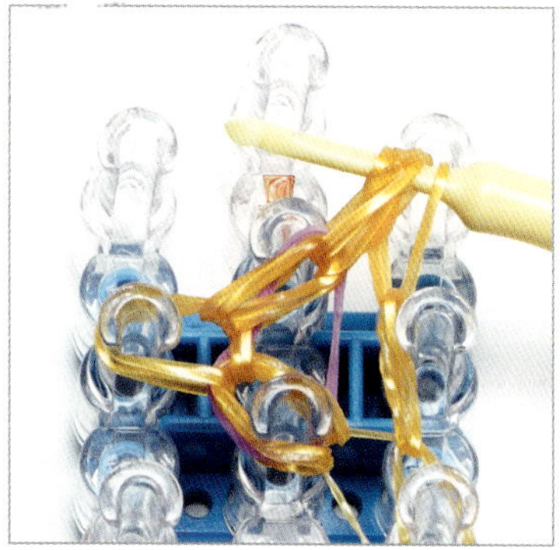

8 When you get to the end of the loom, put your hook through all the bands and slide them off the peg and onto your hook.

9 Pull the first half of your crown off the loom, keeping the end of it on your hook.

10 Now, place the remaining bands on the loom, making sure the arrow is facing away from you when doing so. However, this time, instead of placing gold band 13, stretch the bands off your hook and onto the peg where it would have been.

11 Repeat steps 1-9, starting at the first peg in the right-hand row, where you just placed the first half of your crown.

12 Slide your clip onto the bands currently on your hook, then slide both loops of the last band at the other end of the chain into the clip as well. Your crown is now complete! You may need to extend it, depending on your head size. If so, use the guidance on p3 to help.

Headband Project Two

Festival Garland

For this project you'll need:

- ✔ 10 pink bands
- ✔ 10 purple bands
- ✔ 10 yellow bands
- ✔ 10 orange bands
- ✔ 59 green bands
- ✔ 1 clip
- ✔ 1 pencil

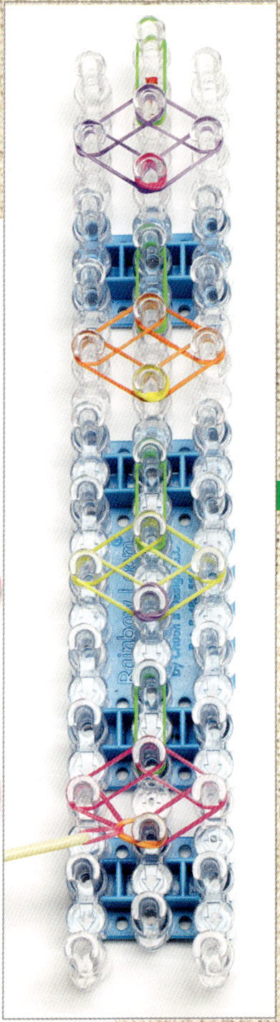

Setting up your loom!

Set up your loom in the STAGGERED configuration, making sure the arrow is facing away from you, then place the bands in the order shown in diagram 1. You're going to have to do this twice, to make eight flowers for your garland.

1 Turn your loom so the arrow is facing towards you. With this design, you're going to be looping the bands in reverse order to how they were placed, starting at orange band 24. So, putting your hook inside this peg, push back the top orange band, hook the top pink band and loop it diagonally to the upper left-hand peg, where it originated from.

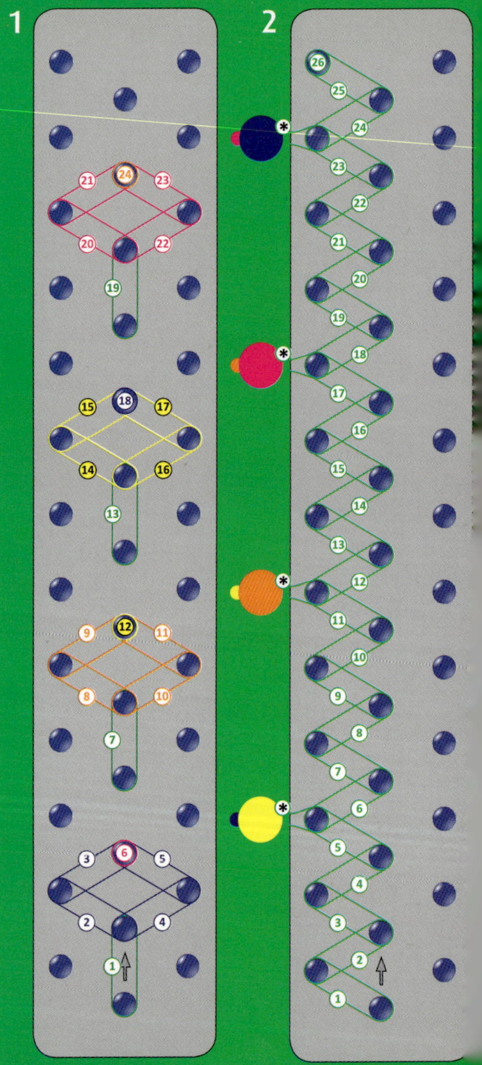

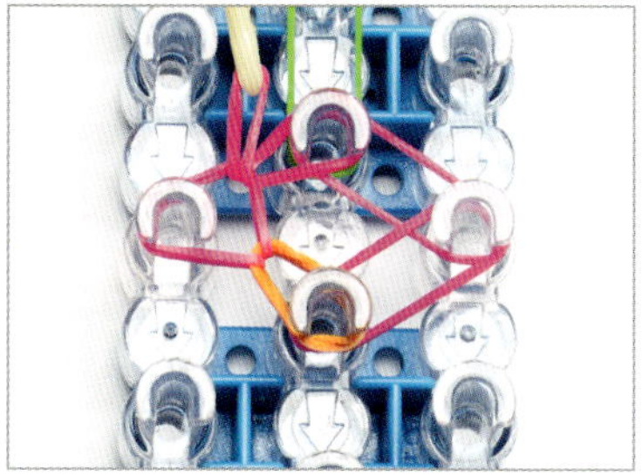

2 Put your hook in the peg you just finished on, reach the bottom pink band and loop it diagonally to the upper central peg.

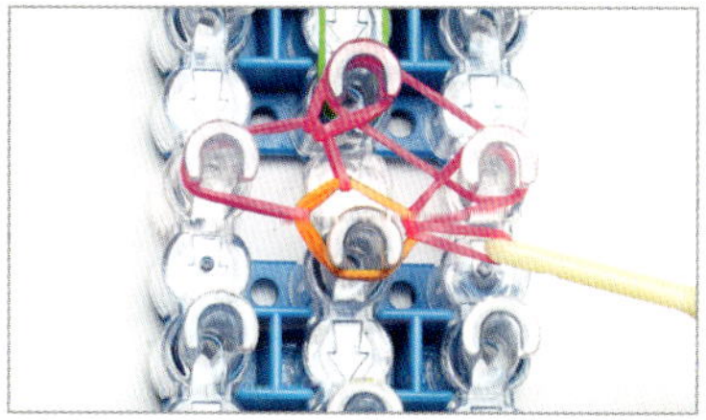

3 Going back to the first peg, push back the top orange band, catch the bottom pink band and loop it diagonally to the upper right-hand peg.

4 At the peg you just looped to, hook the bottom pink band and loop it diagonally to the upper central row.

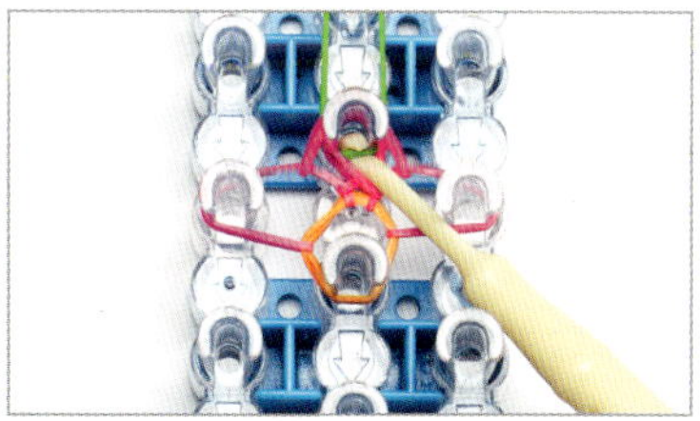

5 Putting your hook in the peg you just finished on, reach down and catch the green band from the bottom and loop forward.

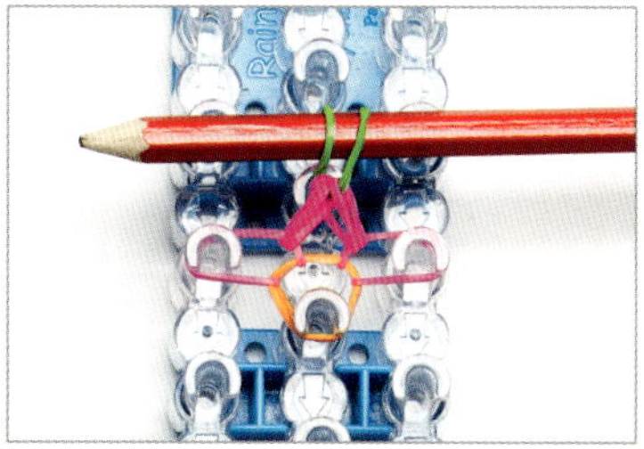

6 Now, taking a pen or pencil, slide the two ends of the green band off the peg and onto your pencil for storage. This is your first flower.

7 Repeat steps 1-6 to create three more flowers.

8 Now, place more bands on the loom as in diagram 1 and repeat steps 1-7, so that you have a total of eight flowers stored on your pencil.

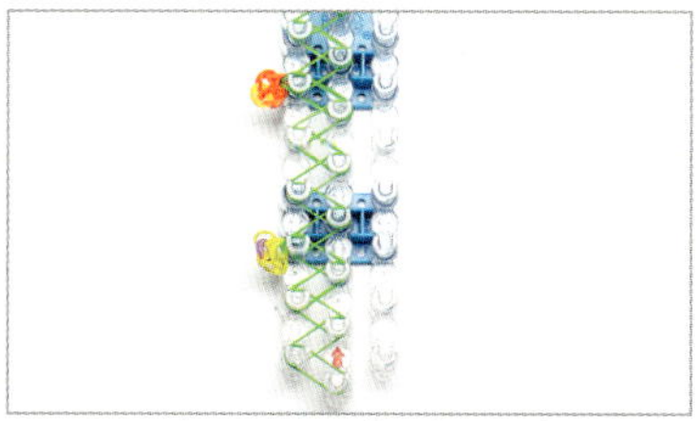

9 Next, place 26 green bands as in diagram 2 (making sure the loom arrow is facing away from you when doing so). At each point marked with a star, carefully stretch a flower off the storage pencil and onto the peg. Make sure both ends of the green band go firmly over the peg.

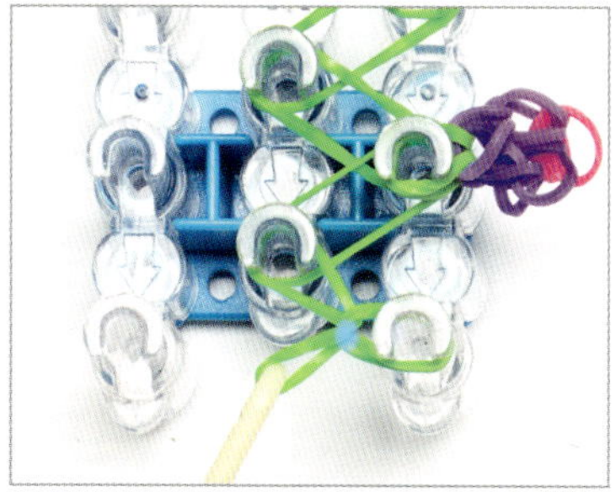

10 You're now ready to start looping the first half of your chain. Making sure your loom arrow is facing you, put your hook inside the peg with green band 26 around it, push it back, catch the bottom green band and loop it diagonally to the upper left-hand side.

11 Keep on hooking and looping all the green bands in the chain in a zigzag pattern, until you reach the end of the loom. Make sure you always hook the bottom band from inside the peg.

12 Now, slide your last band ends off the last peg and onto your hook. Keeping it on your hook, pull the whole thing off the loom and put it to one side.

13 Now, place the remaining 25 green bands on the loom, as in diagram 2 (making sure the loom arrow is facing away from you when doing so). Place your remaining four flowers as before; however, this time, instead of band 26, stretch both the band ends off the hook and onto the peg where band 26 would have been.

14 You're now ready to start looping the second half of your chain. Making sure your loom arrow is facing you, put your hook inside the first peg, push back the top bands, catch the bottom green band and loop it diagonally to the upper left-hand side.

13 Keep on hooking and looping all the green bands in the chain in a zigzag pattern until you reach the end of the loom. Make sure you always hook just the bottom band from inside the peg.

14 Now, slide the band ends off the last peg and onto your hook. Attach them together with a clip, then pull the whole thing off the loom. Slide the green band at the other end of the chain into the clip as well to complete your festival garland!

Headband Project Three

Bow Hair Clip

For this project you'll need:

- ✓ 8 yellow bands
- ✓ 20 mixed coloured bands
- ✓ 1 hair clip

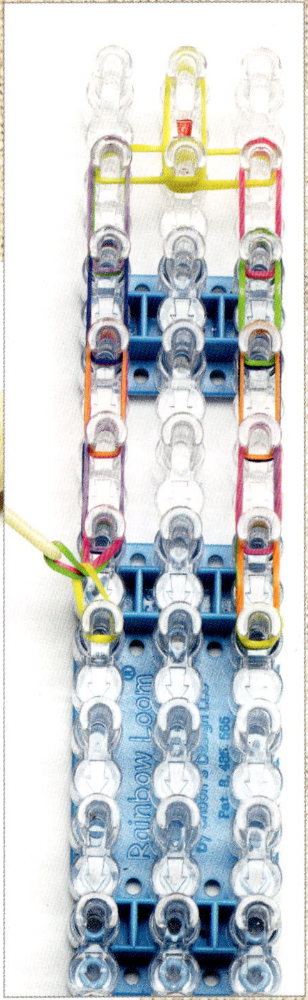

Setting up your loom!

Set up your loom in the SQUARED configuration, making sure the arrow is facing away from you, then place the bands in the order shown in the diagram.

1 Turn your loom so the arrow is facing towards you. With this design, you're going to be looping the bands in reverse order to how they were placed, starting at yellow band 28. So, putting your hook inside this peg, push back the top yellow band, hook the bottom pair of coloured bands down and loop them forward.

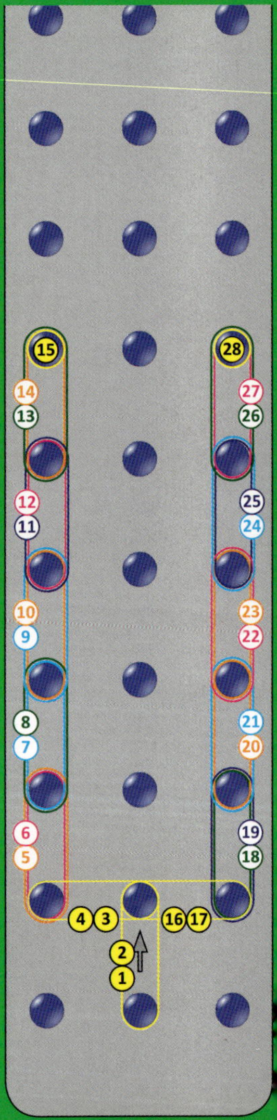

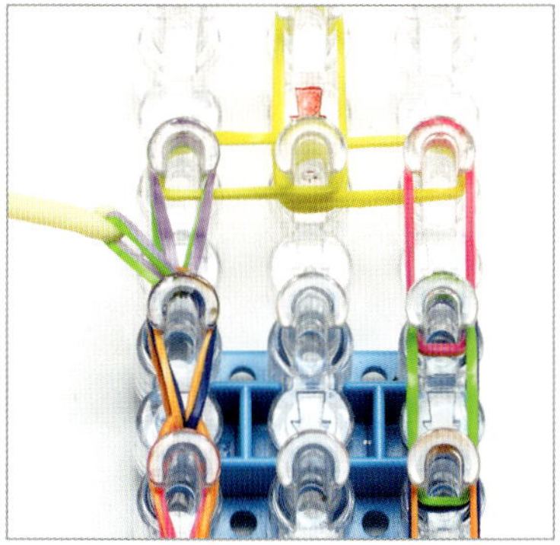

2 Continue hooking and looping the next four pairs of coloured bands forward, each time making sure you take from inside the peg.

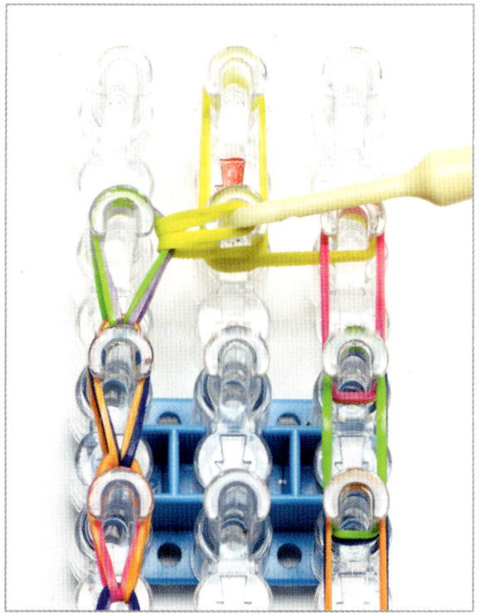

3 When you get to the next pair, which are yellow, you're going to hook them as normal, from inside the pegs, but this time loop them directly to the right, on to the central row.

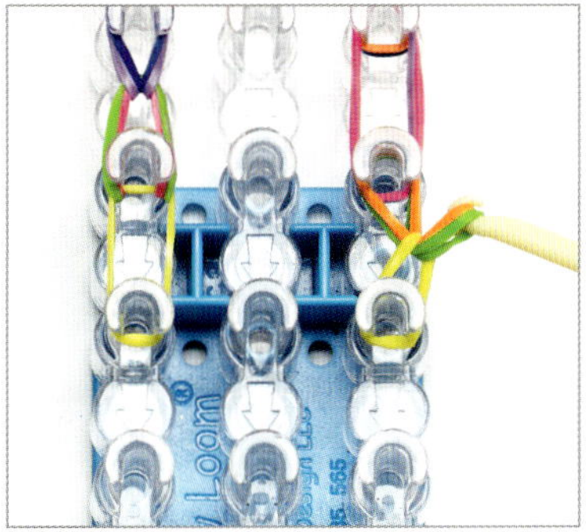

4 Now, repeat steps 1-3 on the right-hand side, starting at yellow band 15.

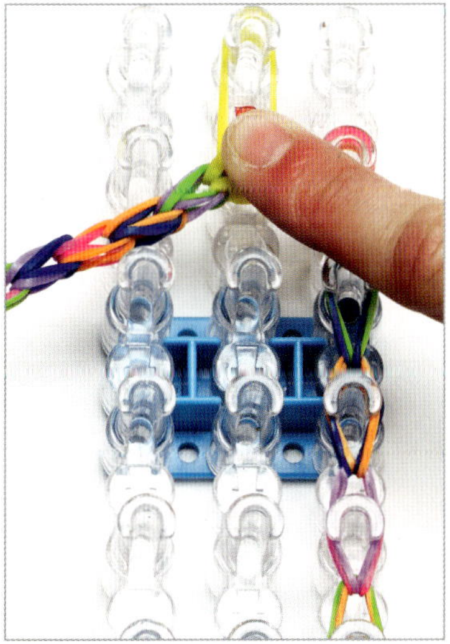

5 Keeping your finger on the central peg you just finished on to stop the last yellow band coming off the loom, pull the looped coloured band chain off the loom.

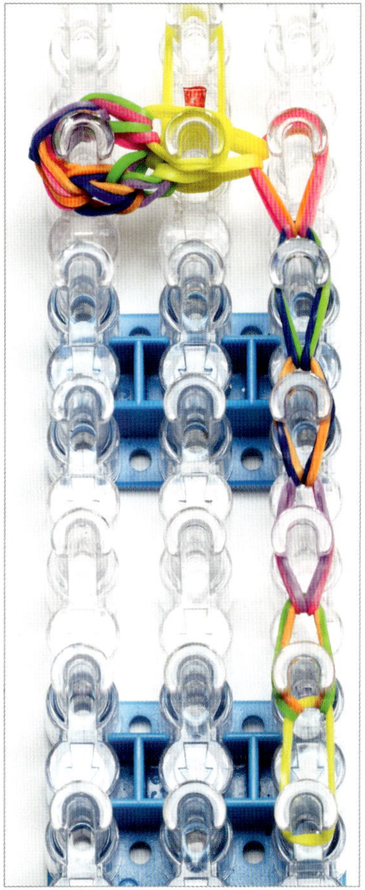

6 Stretch both loops of the first yellow band over that central peg.

7 Repeat step 6 on the left-hand side. Both sides of your bow are now formed.

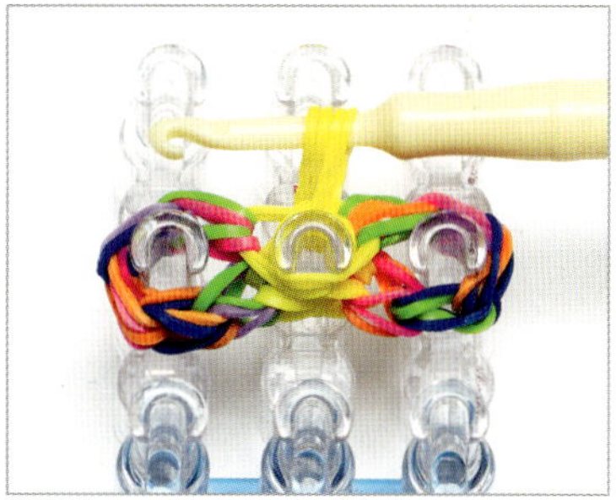

8 Now, putting your hook in the peg you just finished on, hook the bottom pair of yellow bands forward. Put your hook through them both and pull your bow off the loom.

9 Take your hair clip and slide one side of it through both loops of the bands currently on your hook.

Your hair clip is complete and ready to wear!

These look great as a matching set – why not try making several of them for a really cute hairstyle? You can try them with any number of colours, and for a simpler look you can replace the mixed coloured bands with just one colour!

Headband Project Four

Teddy Bear Ears

For this project you'll need:

- ✓ 66 brown bands
- ✓ 12 pink bands
- ✓ 1 headband

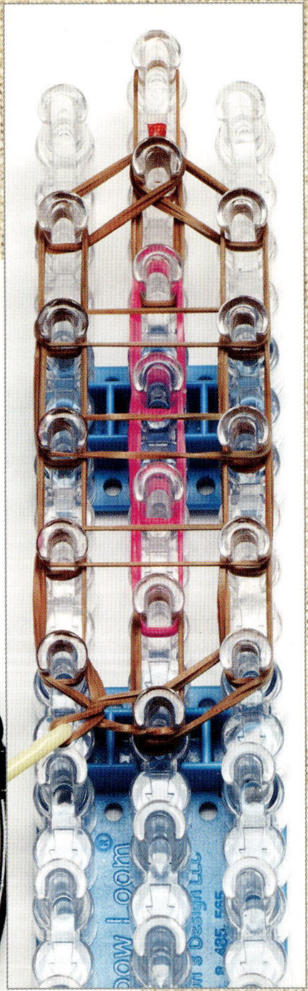

Setting up your loom!

Set up your loom in the STAGGERED configuration, making sure the arrow is facing away from you, then place the bands in the order shown in the diagram. You're going to have to do this twice, to make two teddy bear ears.

1 Turn your loom so the arrow is facing towards you. With this design, you're going to be looping the bands in reverse order to how they were placed, starting at brown band 36. So, putting your hook inside this peg, push back the top brown band, hook the next pair of brown bands down and loop them diagonally to the upper left-hand peg, where they originate from.

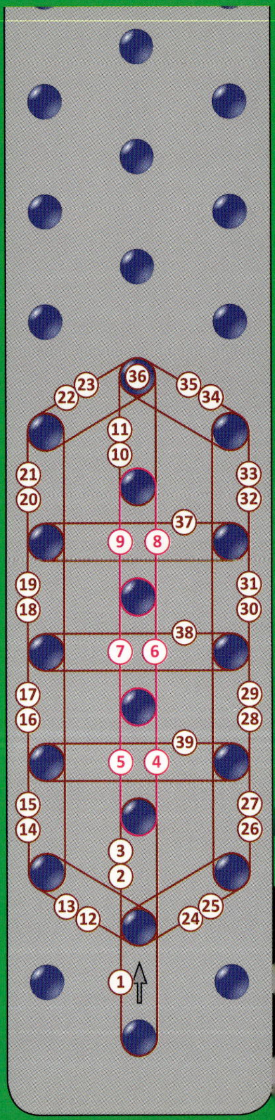